PAN'INO *veggie*

Alessandro Frassica

veggie
PAN'INO

photographs by Irene Berni

Guido Tommasi Editore

Contents

Nutrition: substance and spirit

This is a wide and much debated topic.
What we eat is a reflection of our true identity; our
tastes, our weaknesses and our virtues.
The relationship we have with food accompanies us throughout
our life: it is an experience that is integral to ourselves and
which can be interpreted in the most varied ways.
When we are born; our mother's milk is the first food that nourishes us,
and from that point on we begin our journey, along with our education and
the context in which we live (geographical area, traditions, religion...).
As we grow up, we gradually acquire greater knowledge, we get to know
ourselves better, and in doing so we work towards meeting our needs, initially
concentrating on taste, then on what makes us healthy inside and out.
Therefore, nutrition also becomes an approach to health and well-being.
The human body depends on what we eat, from the quality of the food,
and from everything that is compatible with the needs of our organism.
We choose, combine, and transform our nutrition;
in this way substance becomes spirit.
Nutrition is thus a source of nourishment for pleasure; the taste of the quality of
the ingredients, their preparation and combinations, but also, and above all, it is a
source of benefit to our health and a source of energy for our bodies and minds.
Finally, nutrition is prevention and cure for illnesses and tumours; an aspect which
conditions our spirits and our lifestyle, because our body reacts in different ways
according to how and what we eat.
Therefore, a correct philosophy of nutrition guarantees us excellent health,
vitality and well-being.

Flour

Wholemeal flour must be TRULY whole.
It must be ground using a traditional stone. This allows the grinding of the grain in a single process, which maintains all the elements that nature has decided to include in the grain. Flour ground in this way is rich in trace elements, mineral salts, water-soluble vitamins, and contains live wheat germ, one of the most important parts of the grain, that is usually removed and, if replaced, is stabilised (using thermal treatment).

Traditional millstones differ from those on the market today; they turn very slowly and are chiselled by hand periodically by the miller.
This creates the right surface for the milling of the cereal without overheating it, thus maintaining the grain and flour at a very low temperature. This is a vital element because if the grain is too warm, the vitamins and other nutrients are lost and the flour has a tendency to turn rancid easily. The maintenance of the millstone is a long practiced art that requires great experience, but has almost been lost.

In an ideal world all flour would be certified organic, or at the very least from cereal-producing farmers who did not use weed killers, pesticides, fungicides or chemical fertilisers.

Before being ground, all cereals must undergo a long process consisting of various stages from an initial cleaning of the drain, for the storage of clean grains, at a controlled temperature in order to eliminate the formation of mould and prevent insect contamination. The last step is cleaning by way of an optical selector, the latest technology that can photograph every single grain and select the good grains from those that are defective in order to grind only top quality materials that are absolutely pure and safe for food use. Finally, crop rotation of the land is very important, so that the same product is never sown every year; in this way the land remains fertile and the plants are able to obtain nitrogen in a naturally.

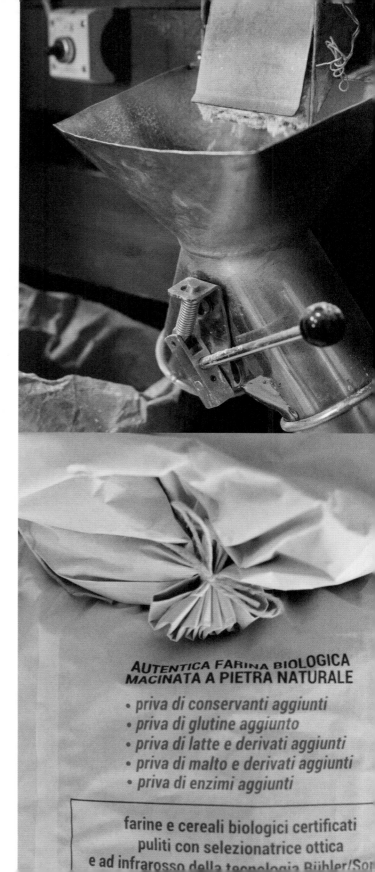

AUTENTICA FARINA BIOLOGICA
MACINATA A PIETRA NATURALE

- priva di conservanti aggiunti
- priva di glutine aggiunto
- priva di latte e derivati aggiunti
- priva di malto e derivati aggiunti
- priva di enzimi aggiunti

farine e cereali biologici certificati
puliti con selezionatrice ottica
e ad infrarosso della tecnologia Bühler/Sor

'ino's recipes

2 slices of smoked
scamorza cheese

few escarole
lettuce leaves

2 slices of
fig bread

Bello de casa
A homemade delight

Wash and roughly chop the escarole lettuce, then put it in a hot
pan together with the carefully rinsed Muscat grapes. When
the escarole has softened, turn off the heat and place
the slices of scamorza on top. As soon as they
begin to melt with the heat put everything
on a warmed slice of bread and sprinkle with
crushed hazelnuts.

8-10 Muscat
grapes

Close the sandwich and take a bite: the bitter notes of
the escarole combine with the sweetness of the Muscat
grapes, the smokiness and softness of the scamorza and
the toasted crunchy texture of the hazelnuts. The vegan
version without cheese is also excellent.

A play on combinations which is used in various recipes, above all in
Southern Italy, which we have interpreted in our own way...

3-4
hazelnuts

24

Caprino

2 slices of bread made with Enkir flour

60 g robiola goat's cheese

2-3 slices of grilled pepper

2-3 grilled marinated courgettes

5-6 mint leaves

Cut three slices of robiola, each one a couple of centimetres thick, and place on a slice of bread, then put into a hot oven, just until the cheese begins to melt, but be careful not to overheat it! Then take the pepper slices and the marinated courgettes (in extra-virgin olive oil and aromatic herbs) and lay them on the cheese with the mint leaves. Close the sandwich with another slice of warmed bread.

Take a bite and you will be hit by a truly intriguing combination of flavours.

Robiola goat's cheese is the main ingredient of this panino, a cheese that I adore, both fresh with more acidic notes, and a little mature, when it becomes more intense and captivating.

Wow, what a panino!

2 slices of bread with sultanas, made with type 2 Buratto flour
1 green Savoy cabbage leaf
1 ½ cabbage leaf
½ an avocado
1 dessertspoon vegan mayonnaise
1 teaspoon turmeric
1 teaspoon chia seeds
black pepper

**FOR THE VEGAN MAYONNAISE
(FROM A RECIPE BY ARTURO DORI)**
1 piece of root ginger about 2 cm
80 ml soya milk
1 teaspoon Dijon mustard
½ lemon
1 teaspoon vinegar
peanut oil
salt and pepper

Place all the ingredients for the vegan mayonnaise in the container of a handheld food mixer and blend until a smooth frothy mixture is obtained.

Cut the cabbage into thin slices: you can choose whether to use it raw or to cook it briefly in a hot frying pan with a little oil. It is important to maintain its crispness. Cut the avocado into thin slices, then create your panino by layering the various ingredients on a slice of bread: the cabbage, the avocado and the mayonnaise. Sprinkle with turmeric, black pepper and chia seeds then put another slice of bread on the top.

More than just a cabbage panino!

Black pepper is important because it facilitates and increases the assimilation of the extraordinary properties of turmeric.

Turmeric, a bright yellow powder, is one of the main components used in Ayurvedic and traditional Indian medicine because of its therapeutic purifiying properties. It is particularly indicated in the case of digestive and liver problems. It has antitumoural effects due to its principal component curcumin, which are recognised and appreciated.

Leafy cabbages, dense and without inflorescence like the Savoy cabbage, the common cabbage and red cabbage are all excellent sources of iron, vitamins A and C, folic acid and other antitumoural substances.

Chips.

Take the cabbage leaves, remove the central core, roughly chop into chips and cook briefly in a pan with very hot oil. When they are crispy, place them on the bread and add the dandelion, radishes, radish roots, linseeds, and a pinch of whole salt. Top the panino with another slice of bread.

Taraxacum officinale, better known as dandelion, is used for its depurative properties. It is gathered when it is still a shoot and preserved in oil. You will discover the delightfulness of this panino in its play on flavours but above all, in its textures and contrasts. "Delicious"!

2 slices of rye bread

extra-virgin olive oil, for frying

Maremma whole salt

1 teaspoon linseeds

3 red cabbage leaves

1 handful of dandelions

2 thinly sliced raw radishes

a few radish roots

1 carrot

2 salad leaves

1 dessertspoon chickpea and rosemary cream

2 slices of bread made with type 2 Buratto flour

a couple of yellow and purple cauliflower heads

1 teaspoon pumpkin seeds

1 teaspoon horseradish sauce

extra-virgin olive oil, for frying

32

Colour

Remove the stems from the cauliflower heads, keeping only the tops. Fry briefly in a pre-heated pan with a drizzle of extra-virgin olive oil, but do not overcook them: they need to remain very crunchy. Lightly toast the pumpkin seeds.

I have used a rather funny utensil (spiralizer) to cut the carrots: with the shape of a large pencil sharpener, in which you insert the raw carrot, which then comes out as a curl, with the shape and texture of a leaf. So, just right for a panino!

Cut two slices of bread and spread the chick pea cream on one of them, then add the fried cauliflower, the pumpkin seeds, the sliced carrot on which you have evenly spread the horseradish sauce, and the salad leaves. Top with the other slice of bread.

At this point your mouth will already be watering... and while you take a bite of this panino and taste it, you will feel as if you are not only eating something excellent but also full of goodness!

Horseradish sauce is derived from *armoracia rusticana*, a wild pungent root that has a similar taste to that of wasabi but more delicate. It is excellent with many vegetables; with raw carrot it is simply magical.

The colours that this panino emanates speak for themselves: nature is truly incredible. Even if just for this reason, working with vegetables is really entertaining.

Fabulous

Spread the gorgonzola on one of the slices of bread and warm in the oven until the cheese begins to melt. In the meantime, lightly fry the thinly sliced sprouts in a pan, crumble the walnuts and mix all these ingredients. If you wish to heighten the acid element in order to create a contrast with the sweetness of the gorgonzola, add a few drops of balsamic vinegar.

Brussels sprouts represent a fantastic food for the prevention of tumours, provided they are not overcooked.

A couple of walnuts a day are a real cure-all: they contain vitamin E, omega 3, phytosterols, and flavenoids. They have preventative anti-cholesterol power and they are a barrier against the formation of tumour cells.

2 slices of
walnut bread

2
walnuts

60 g sweet
gorgonzola

2 Brussels
sprouts

Fig-issimo
Awesome!

Cut the bread, add a generous layer of creamy gorgonzola and pop it into a hot oven just until the cheese begins to melt. Remove from the oven and spread the mustard on so that it combines with the warm gorgonzola.
Close the sandwich and close your eyes, too: a good bite, and a whole new world will appear!

A panino that is one of the most highly rated and appreciated by 'ino.

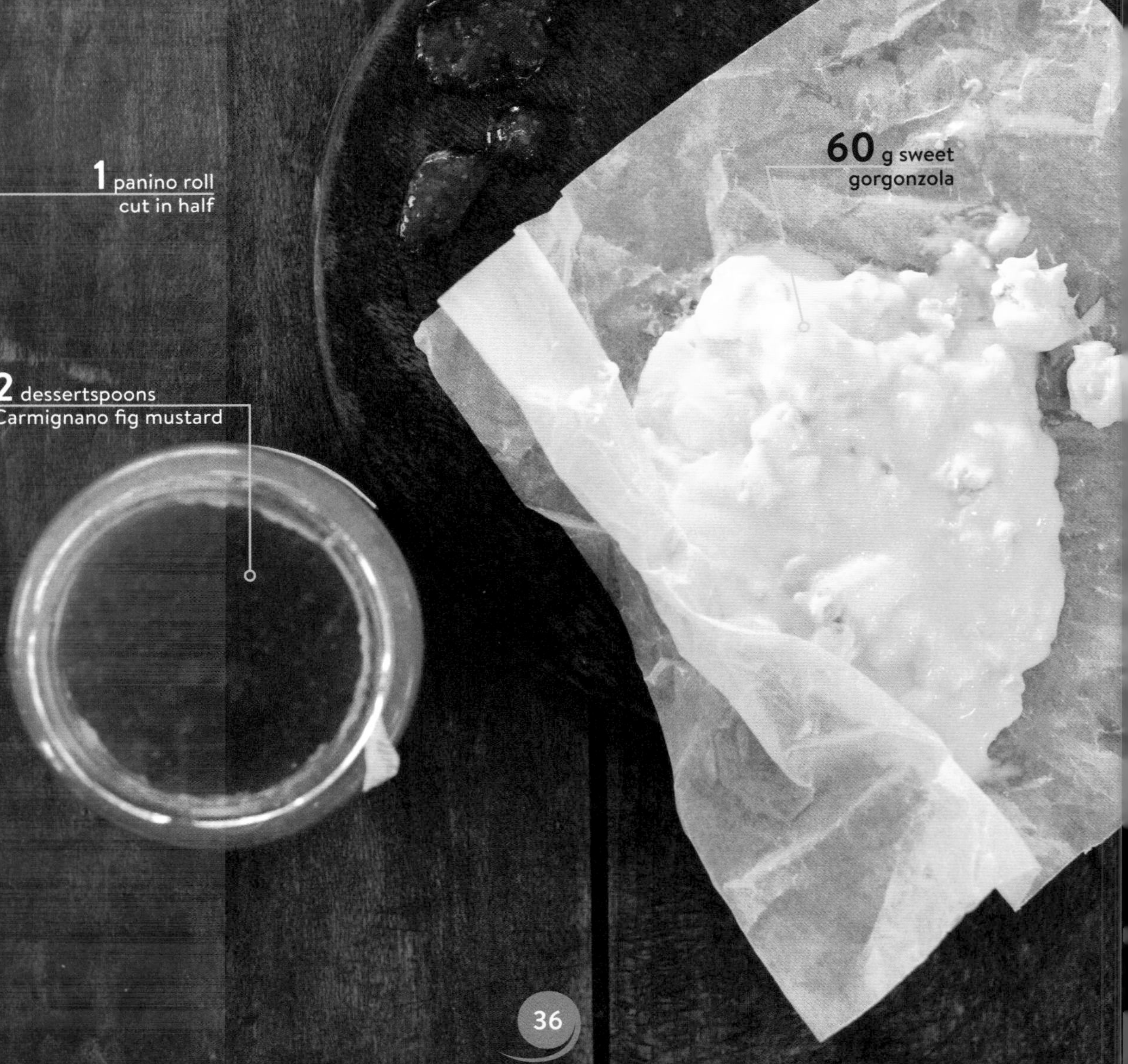

1 panino roll
cut in half

2 dessertspoons
Carmignano fig mustard

60 g sweet
gorgonzola

Two magnificent ingredients that together become incredible:
a perfect marriage.
Carmignano is a town in the hills around Prato, famous for
its good wine and for its delicious dried figs. This heavenly
fig mustard is made from these particular figs with the
addition of a few mustard seeds.

*Yellow*Red

1 wholemeal roll cut in half
50 g saffron pecorino
50 g lightly fried spinach
1 dessertspoon pepper chutney

Spread the pecorino on one half of the roll.
Gently warm, then add the chutney and a layer of
fresh spinach, which you have previously lightly
fried so as to keep all its crispiness intact.

A combination of unusual flavours: with just the
right sweetness at the beginning and a pleasing
spicy note at the end.

"Yum!"

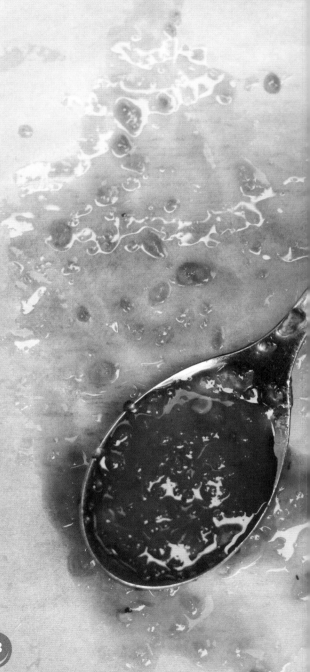

The colours and the aesthetic aspect of this panino have an enormous impact. Saffron pecorino is obtained by macerating saffron stems from San Gimignano in milk from the Crete Senesi... a truly superb product.

Hamburger'ino

You can make the omelette in the frying pan or in the oven. Add a few shreds of red cabbage leaves to the eggs; the omelette needs to be quite high, roughly a couple of centimetres. Then, using a pasta mould, you can make the right shape omelette for the burger bun.

Gently heat the two halves of the burger bun: on one half, place a slice of pecorino, allowing it to melt slowly. On the other, spread a layer of ketchup and add the salad leaf, the slice of tomato and the omelette, then finally the remaining cheese. Close together and... truly delicious!

1 hamburger bun
with seeds

1 dessertspoon
organic ketchup

1 slice of
tomato

1 salad
leaf

1 omelette with
red cabbage

50 g Marzolino
pecorino

A prestigious game: an omelette becomes a hamburger.

I adore an omelette burger: it has been one of my favourites since my childhood. Here we present it in a novel way.

1 handful of
mint leaves

grated zest of 1
organic lemon

1 handful of
basil leaves

50 g stracciatella
burrata (fresh
mozzarella cheese
with cream)

2 slices of seeded
wholemeal bread

1 layer of grilled
marinated courgettes

Place the ingredients on one of the
two slices of bread. Begin with the
courgettes, sprinkled with the
lemon zest, and follow with the
stracciatella cheese and the
aromatic herbs. Top with
the other slice of
bread.

I adore stracciatella cheese. I find it a lustful ingredient. The grilled courgettes make an excellent accompaniment and the addition of mint and basil provides a wonderful aromatic freshness that, with the magic touch of the lemon, completes the harmony and complexity of this extremely tasty but simple sandwich. "I love it!".

Homegrown

Spread each slice of bread with mayonnaise (for the preparation, see the *"Wow, what a panino!"* recipe). Place layers of aubergines, courgettes and turnip greens on one slice, then add the seeds, the Jerusalem artichoke (almost as if it were truffles) and the spirulina. Top with the other slice of bread and be ready to eat a sandwich that will surprise you with its goodness and nutritional properties.

2 slices of seeded bread made with type 2 Buratto flour

3 dessertspoons turnip greens, lightly fried

some grated Jerusalem artichoke

1 handful of mixed linseeds and pumpkin seeds

1 courgette, sliced, grilled and marinated

1 aubergine, sliced, grilled and marinated

2 g powdered spirulina

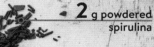

2 dessertspoons vegan mayonnaise

Spirulina is a spiral-shaped microalga, green, almost blue in colour, which reproduces itself through photosynthesis, like plants. Compared with meat, fish and cheese, which contain 20% protein, or legumes and eggs, which contain 13%, spirulina boasts an incredible 70%, already converted from protein into amino acids. It is a 100% vegetable nutraceutical food, and one of the most complete and balanced foods existing in nature. Together with its extremely high protein content, it has an exceptional concentration of vitamins (B, D, E, K), minerals (calcium, magnesium, iron, potassium, zinc, copper, manganese, chrome and selenium), essential amino acids (an astounding 8) and betacarotene.

Spirulina is an antioxidant which reinforces the immune system, fights anaemia, purifies and detoxifies the organism. It is ideal for vegans, vegetarians and coeliacs. In addition, it increases physical resistance and muscle development due to its leucine, isoleucine and valine content. It heightens intellectual concentration and has beneficial effects on skin and hair structure; it is also useful for post-operative convalescence; it is filling (and thus ideal for slimming diets). It grows in fresh water and does not contain iodine, so it is recommended for those who have thyroid problems. The daily assumption of spirulina is recommended for those who have a diet that is low in protein, for anaemia sufferers, sportspeople and those wishing to lose weight.

2 dessertspoons
kale pesto

2 slices rye
bread

50 g fresh
Maremma pecorino
cheese

6-8 toasted
caramelised almonds

For the caramelised almonds
125 ml water
175 g sugar

Take me

For the pesto, see Arturo Dori's recipe on p. 65.

Toast the almonds in the oven. Put the water and
sugar in a pan and keep on heat until the sugar begins
to thicken, then add the almonds and fry quickly.
The caramelising must be very light, and thus brief. I
recommend that you mix well.

Put the fresh pecorino on one of the slices of bread: its
sweetness will contrast with the slightly bitter aroma of
the pesto that you will spread over the cheese.
Roughly chop the almonds and spread them evenly.
Their light sweetness and lovely crunchiness will
combine with the other ingredients to make a winning
combination.

There is so much of Tuscany in this sandwich.

Kale is one of the best-loved winter vegetables. I adore it, and in this recipe we are using its pesto, which means we can enjoy it even out of season.

5 semi-dried cherry tomatoes marinated in extra-virgin olive oil and aromatic herbs

1 handful of powdered Pantelleria capers

50 g sheep ricotta cheese

1 handful Pantelleria oregano

extra-virgin olive oil, for seasoning

1 roll cut in half, black bread from Castelvetrano is recommended

South

Warm the bread in the oven. If you can find it, you can use black bread of Castelvetrano. Spread the ricotta on one slice of bread, then add the cherry tomatoes and sprinkle with oregano and caper powder. Season to taste with a drizzle of extra-virgin olive oil.

These ingredients remind me of our beloved South: the freshness of the ricotta, the intense flavour of the cherry tomatoes, the aroma of capers and oregano.
Simplicity and taste combine in Mediterranean harmony!

Summer

The theme of this sandwich is yogurt, which binds the other ingredients. Slice the cucumber, tomato and the avocado then mix together adding the basil, mint and pumpkin seeds which have been toasted in a pan with a pinch of whole salt. I like to add a little oil and a dusting of Habanero hot chilli pepper.

This is high summer! A panino that you would happily eat on the beach, under the beach umbrella, gazing at the sea...

2 slices of walnut bread

extra-virgin olive oil, for seasoning

1 dusting of Habanero hot chilli pepper (if desired)

whole salt

½ avocado

1 handful of pumpkin seeds

1 fresh tomato

2 basil leaves

2 dessertspoons Greek yogurt

2 mint leaves

1 cucumber

50

Sicily

1 handful of
broad beans

1 dessertspoon almond
and caper pesto

2 slices of bread
made with Enkir flour

50 g pecorino
cheese

1 handful
toasted almonds

1 dessertspoonful
extra-virgin olive oil

1 sprinkling de-salted, dried and
crumbled Pantelleria capers

For the pesto: grind together a few capers, some almonds, a drop of extra-virgin olive oil and, if you wish, a couple of basil leaves, in a mortar and pestle or with an electric handwhisk. The consistency should not be too runny.
Spread the pesto on one slice of bread, cover with roughly chopped almonds, add the beans and lay on a couple of slices of fresh pecorino. Finish with the powdered capers, which give an incredible aroma. A drizzle of oil on the other slice will not fail to please...
Close the sandwich and bite into this piece of Sicily!

Tricolor

5 semi-dried cherry tomatoes marinated in exta-virgin olive oil and aromatic herbs

3 slices of Campana buffalo mozzarella

2 dessertspoons fresh Genoese pesto

1 roll cut in half

Warm the bread in the oven and fill it with 2 cm slices of mozzarella. Add the cherry tomatoes and spread all the ingredients with pesto. I prefer dried seeds because they have a more tender consistency which makes them easier to chew.

For the fresh Genoese pesto:

50 g Genoese basil leaves
20 g pine nuts
80 g Reggiano parmesan cheese
20 g Sardinian pecorino DOP
1 clove garlic
80-100 ml extra-virgin olive oil
1 g large grain salt

White, red and green, long live the Tricolor!

An ever popular super classic whose appeal will never fade.

2 baby onions in balsamic vinegar

1 pepper

1 handful toasted caramelised hazelnuts

1 handful sesame and pumpkin seeds

1 roll cut in half

1 grilled courgette

Green

Spread the broccoli cream on one slice of bread, add the turnip greens – very finely sliced so as to chew them better, then lightly fried – and follow with a layer of courgette, a layer of pepper, then add the halved baby onions and the lettuce or wild salad leaves. Roughly chop the caramelised hazelnuts (see the recipe on p. 46) and the sesame and pumpkin seeds, then evenly spread them on the top. Close the sandwich.

2 lettuce or wild salad leaves

1 handful turnip greens

1 dessertspoon Santa Massenza broccoli cream

What is there to say? A 100% vegetable world in one bite: a source of super-healthy nutritious ingredients!

This is a completely vegetable based roll with many interesting ingredients.

Let's begin with the **Santa Massenza broccoli**, which I came to know thanks to my dear crazy friend Noris, who gathers herbs in the mountains, works with them naturally, creating exceptional pure products. This variety of broccoli is native to the area of Santa Massenza in Trentino; it is cultivated in fields which are fertilised with grape stalks and has a lovely intense flavour with sweetish notes.

The nutritional importance of the hazelnuts is due to their high vitamin content, especially vitamins E and B6, and also mineral salts (copper, iron, manganese and calcium). In addition, they contain a good dose of fibre, and if eaten in moderation they have antioxidant properties.

Vitamin

A classic winter sandwich: thinly slice the fennel and orange, saving their juices, and put them to marinate in extra-virgin olive oil with a pinch of pepper and the orange juice (you could, if you wish, add a little whole salt). Dry and fill the sandwich, adding the crumbled bitter almonds.

Almonds *are rich in magnesium, iron, potassium, copper and vitamin E. Three bitter almonds a day provide a notable antitumoural effect.*

½ fennel bulb

3 bitter almonds

2 slices of walnut bread

½ an orange

extra-virgin olive oil

freshly milled black pepper

1 pinch whole salt (if desired)

Saffron

For the mash
1 courgette
5 saffron threads
2 dessertspoons extra-virgin olive oil
1 dessertspoon parmesan
1 dessertspoon finely chopped walnuts and pine nuts

1 roll, cut in half

4 mint or basil leaves (if desired)

3 dessertspoons courgette and saffron mash

3 slices of scamorza cheese, white or smoked as preferred

Crush the courgette with the extra-virgin olive oil and the saffron threads. As desired, to heighten the taste, you can also add a dessertspoon of grated Reggiano parmesan and a spoonful of finely chopped walnuts and pine nuts.

Lay the scamorza cheese on one half of the roll. You can choose to use either the white variety, which is more delicate or the smoked variety if you prefer a stronger flavour. Place this in the oven until the cheese begins to melt, without overheating or worse, burning.

Remove from the oven, spread the mixture on the top and close the roll with the other half. If you like, you can add a couple of mint or basil leaves: they would combine very well and add a touch of aroma and freshness.

This demonstrates how you can create a tasty panino that is truly extraordinary, with two simple ingredients!

Friends' recipes

Arturo Dori, *personal chef*

Kale pesto, sun-dried tomato, burrata and pine nut panino

4 sun-dried tomatoes (see recipe)

burrata lucana – a select mozzarella curd cheese.

1 dessertspoon pine nuts

1 ciabatta roll or two slices of another type of bread of your choosing

extra-virgin olive oil, for seasoning

salt and pepper

1 dessertspoon kale pesto (see recipe)

Spread the kale pesto on one side of the ciabatta (or on one slice of bread), then add the burrata, the sun-dried tomatoes and the pine nuts.
Season with a drizzle of extra-virgin olive oil, salt and pepper.

Kale pesto

1 bunch of kale
1 small clove garlic
salt and pepper
½ glass extra-virgin olive oil

Tear off the kale leaves to eliminate the central stem, wash them and boil in plenty of salted water (which you will then put aside).
Depending on the period of picking, kale can require different cooking times (average 15 minutes).
Drain and cool immediately in water and ice in order to stop it cooking and fix its colour.
Put the leaves in a food processor with the oil, a little salt, pepper and the pealed garlic clove. Mix until a smooth homogeneous cream is obtained.
If the pesto seems too dry, add some of the cooking water, a little at a time.
It will keep in the fridge for about 5 days, and can be used as a sauce for pasta or with ricotta ravioli, in addition to this recipe.

Sun-dried tomatoes

100 g sun-dried tomatoes
½ cup extra-virgin olive oil
1 dessertspoon oregano
1 dessertspoon capers, previously de-salted in cold water
1 clove garlic

Place the sun-dried tomatoes to soak in hot water for at least two hours until they are rehydrated and become soft. Then drain and squeeze them out, and dry them on kitchen towel.
Put the tomatoes in a bowl and add the other ingredients. Mix well and leave to rest in the fridge for a day before using them.
If they are well-dried, these tomatoes can be preserved in the fridge for over two weeks.

Arturo Dori

*Kale pesto, sun-dried tomato,
burrata and pine nut panino*

Enrica Della Martira, *chef by passion*

Wholemeal ciabatta with roast pumpkin, Seggiano pecorino and lime blossom honey

300 g
pumpkin

3 thin slices fresh
Seggiano pecorino

1 dessertspoon
lime blossom honey

1 dessertspoon
pumpkin seeds

1 small ciabatta
roll

extra-virgin olive
oil, for seasoning

salt and
pepper

1 sprig
rosemary

Cut the pumpkin into slices of 2/3 mm without eliminating the skin,
place on a tray covered with greaseproof paper and season with a
pinch of salt and pepper, and the finely chopped rosemary. Bake at
150°C for about 20 minutes. In the meantime, toast the pumpkin
seeds in a small pan for a few minutes. When the pumpkin is ready,
take it out of the oven and leave to cool on kitchen paper. Cut the
ciabatta in half, moisten the inside with a drizzle of oil, and place the
pumpkin slices on one half, covering them with the pecorino. Put
both halves of the ciabatta under the grill until the cheese begins
to melt, remove from the oven and add the pumpkin seeds and the
honey on the top of the cheese. Close and bite into it while still hot!

Enrica Della Martira

Wholemeal ciabatta with roast pumpkin,
Seggiano pecorino and lime blossom honey

Enrico Panero
chef of the "DaVinci" restaurant at Eataly, Firenze

Incavolato nero Tuscan kale panino

For the bread:
250 g type 00 flour
110 g strong flour
80 g kale extract
125 ml water
35 g extra-virgin olive oil
3 g baking yeast
4 g honey
15 g salt

For the potato mayonnaise:
100 g boiled potatoes
1 egg yolk
15 g mustard
15 g lemon juice
70 g extra-virgin olive oil

For the tempura:
20 g kale
30 g carrots
20 g celery
30 g Savoy cabbage
20 g onions
80 g type 00 flour
40 g potato flour
40 g rice flour
sparkling water
peanut oil,
for frying

For the cannellini cream:
80 g cannellini beans
30 g extra-virgin olive oil
chilli pepper
salt

Cut the roll in half and remove some of the crumb from both halves. Starting from the base, add a spoonful of cannellini cream, the tempura and the finely chopped raw Savoy cabbage seasoned with oil and salt. Conclude with the mayonnaise and close the roll.

1 dessertspoon raw Savoy cabbage

For the bread: bring together all the liquid ingredients and allow the yeast to dissolve. Add the flour mixed with the salt and kale extract, then make a dough. Allow to rise for about 30 minutes. Form roll shapes and leave to rise for a further 20 minutes. Cook at 200°C for about 25 minutes.

For the tempura: combine the flour and add the sparkling water to create the right consistency. Cut the vegetables into strips, mix together and add the batter. Fry in plenty of peanut oil to create 4 fritters.

For the cannellini cream: put the legumes to soak the night before and then boil them in plenty of water until they are soft.
When they have finished cooking, drain and blend them with extra-virgin olive oil, salt and chilli pepper.

For the potato mayonnaise: cream the potatoes with a handheld mixer, adding the egg yolk, mustard and lemon juice, then drizzle in the extra-virgin olive oil, as you would for a classic mayonnaise.

Enrico Panero

Incavolato nero.
Tuscan kale panino

Giuseppe Calabrese, *journalist and food critic*

Veg. lampredotto
Vegetarian tripe

spirulina

green sauce

vegetarian tripe

spicy soy sauce

1 "rosetta" roll

Cut the rosetta roll in two. On the lower part place a little chopped vegetarian tripe seasoned with green sauce, spicy soy sauce and a little spirulina. Moisten the upper part of the roll with the vegetarian tripe broth and close the roll.

Vegetarian tripe

3 lt water
2 onions
2 carrots
3 celery stalks
50 ml soy sauce
50 g grated root ginger
400 g natural seitan

Wash the vegetables well. Peel the carrots; peel and chop the onions in half, then cut the celery stalks. Put the vegetables in cold water and leave to cook for an hour. Put the seitan in the broth, adding the soy sauce and the ginger. Leave to cook for another hour. Be careful as the seitan may stick to the bottom of the pan at the beginning of cooking, so lift it with a wooden spoon from time to time. After a minute it will begin to float.

Natural seitan

1 kg type 0 flour
550 g water

Knead the flour and water for about 5 minutes. Make a ball shape and put it in a basin covered with water. Leave to rest for eight hours. After this time, drain and work for a few minutes, then rinse under the tap. In this way the starch separates and comes out, colouring the water white. Continue until only a glutinous mass remains, which is the seitan. It will weigh about 400 grammes.

Spicy soy sauce

50 ml soy sauce
3 hot chilli peppers

Leave the chilli peppers to infuse the soy sauce for at least five days. You can increase the spice level by using more chillis.

Green sauce

120 g parsley, 1 dessertspoon salted capers, 50 g vinegar, 100 g extra-virgin olive oil, pepper, 80 g stale bread

Clean the parsley carefully, removing the bigger stems and keeping only the best leaves, then wash, dry and chop it very finely. Remove the salt from the capers and chop very finely. Cut the stale bread, removing the crust, keeping only the crumb. Chop the crumb into cubes and moisten with the vinegar. Squash the crumb to obtain a fine mixture, then add to the parsley and capers. Mix well adding the oil, and then the pepper according to taste. You could use cider vinegar instead of the classic type, or you can add algae to the parsley and capers.

Giuseppe Calabrese

Vegetarian tripe

Irene Berni, *chef and photographer by passion*

Veg breakfast

Cut the figs into thick slices vertically.
Toast the slices of bread and cut in half on the diagonal.
Spread the caprino (or vegrino) on a triangle and cover with slices of figs.
Close with the other slice of bread moistened with syrup.

4 slices of wholemeal bread with 8 cereals

maple syrup

2 figs

50 g caprino goats' cheese or vegrino vegetarian cheese

Vegrino
For a vegan version substitute the caprino cheese with vegrino which is none other than strained soya yogurt.
Add the juice of half a lemon and a pinch of salt to the yogurt.
Place some gauze over a bowl and pour over the seasoned yogurt.
Hold the four corners of the gauze and hang the pouch to strain (in such a way that it does not stay immersed in the buttermilk). For a really good result, wait 24 hours. For the amounts, consider that the final result will be less than half the initial weight, for example from 500 g of yogurt, you will obtain about 210 g of vegrino.

a few chopped
basil leaves

cherry
tomatoes

hazelnuts

salt

flax
seeds

Leonardo Romanelli, *journalist and food critic*

Demons·and·saints·

the juice of
1 lime

onion

extra-virgin
olive oil

1 roll

1 aubergine

some mint leaves

1 handful courgette sticks

Asking the above (who has published a recipe book on offal) for a vegan panino recipe, seemed like provocation on the part of 'ino, and I did not hesitate to provide one. It made me think: it is necessary to think when you decide to become vegan. Creating a flavoursome journey during which you can find characteristics that can regale your palate with intriguing emotions, within foods often unknown or simply forgotten, is a stimulating process. Everything starts with the bread: however ordinary it may be. It has the job of receiving, but also of providing, thanks to its crust, that toasted element which competes with the captivating filling.

A sweet aubergine has been chosen, which should not be too bold, and then comes the decision to smoke it in the oven. Blend the extracted pulp with extra-virgin olive oil and the ripped mint leaves. Add a little salt and place on the bottom half of the roll. Then add the onion, cherry tomatoes, finely chopped courgette sticks and basil. Season with a drop of oil and lime juice, which is not as strong as lemon and more varied in terms of aromas, and the flax seeds warmed in a pan. Conclude with the oven-toasted hazelnuts to guarantee the pleasure of a great crunch that leads to a lasting combined aromatic sensation.

Leonardo·Romanelli

Demons and saints

Luca Cai, *chef of "Il Magazzino" trattoria in Florence*

Vegan 4 "Ps" panino

bread roll

vegan green peppercorn sauce

polenta

peeled piccadilly tomatoes

extra-virgin olive oil, for seasoning

salt and pepper

Cut the bread in half (in this case, a ciabatta) and pop the two halves in the toaster for 2 minutes. Flavour the inside with the green pepper sauce, adding the previously fried or griddled polenta, and finally the tomatoes, extra-virgin olive oil, salt and pepper to taste.

Vegan green peppercorn sauce

celery

carrot

onion

extra-virgin olive oil

green peppercorns

soya cream and rice milk

cooking time: about 90 minutes

Make a mixture of the vegetables in equal parts, gently fry in extra-virgin olive oil and 10% green peppercorns. Complete the cooking with the soya cream and rice milk as for a ragù. Add salt and pepper to taste.

Peeled piccadilly tomatoes

Immerse the tomatoes in boiling water for 1 minute, then peel them and place in a glass jar. Close and allow to boil for 30 minutes, then leave to cool in the fridge.

Polenta

300 g fine wholegrain corn polenta per litre of water

cooking time: about 90 minutes

Polenta takes its origins from the corn of ancient times, which was not irrigated in fields and was very vitreous; the more you cook the polenta, the sweeter and more pleasing it becomes.

Use a thick bottomed pan with a splatter guard to maintain even heat. Heat the water and before it reaches boiling point, gradually pour in the flour, stirring with a whisk to avoid lumps forming. Mix for a few minutes, then lower the flame, cover and mix every now and again, leaving it to cook for the time stated. Pour into a rectangular food container and leave to cool in the fridge.

Luca Cai

Vegan 4 "Ps." panino

Alessia Morabito, *chef*
Paola Mencarelli, *journalist and food critic*

The campagna and riviera panino

6 rolls

200 g natural starter dough
4 g yeast
250 ml water
500 g flour

mock artichoke cheese

600 g artichokes, if possible from the Maremma
1 clove garlic
100 g red onions
20 g parsley
10 g kanten (agar)
100 ml soya milk
1 teaspoon turmeric
1 dessertspoon shoyu
1 dessertspoon soya cream
a pinch of pepper

tarragon pesto

10 g Siena tarragon
1 pinch salt
30 g extra-virgin olive oil

pepper

fried artichokes

1 thin leaf artichoke
1 pinch gomashio
20 g extra-virgin olive oil

chick pea bake

200 g organic chick pea flour
600 g water
6 g salt
125 g extra-virgin olive oil

Work the starter dough, water and yeast together. Add the mixture to the flour, work energetically and then leave to rest for a couple of hours away from draughts.

In the meantime, mix the chick pea flour with the water and salt in a container. Leave to rest.

Put the artichokes, garlic, red onions and parsley to simmer. When they are soft, blend them and remove about 300g of pulp. Mix with the kanten (agar) dissolved in the soya milk, the turmeric, a milling of pepper, the shoyu and the soya cream. Cook rapidly in a small pan, stirring continuously until the mixture comes away from the sides, then place in a mould greased with olive oil.

Form the rolls, lightly flour them on the top and leave to rise for another hour.

Mash the fresh Siena tarragon leaves in a mortar and pestle together with the oil and salt.

Put the rolls in a pre-heated oven at 180°C for 20/25 minutes, then take out.

Heat a baking tray, copper if possible, in the oven. When it is hot, pour on the oil. Make sure it is evenly distributed then pour on the chick pea mixture and cook for 30 minutes at 240°C. Remove and keep warm.

Lightly fry the artichoke leaves with the extra-virgin olive oil and the gomashio, then...

"We are ready to create our roll: divide it in half and spread with the tarragon pesto. Then add the slices of mock artichoke cheese, the hot chick pea bake, a sprinkling of pepper and the lightly fried artichokes. Close and... buon appetito!".

Alessia Morabito and Paola Mencarelli

"We met in the Maremma. It was spring, and there were Pian di Rocca artichokes on the menu", says the chef who grew up between Livorno and Pisa, with the aroma of chick pea bake. "And I suggested that you tried it with tarragon as they do in Siena", replies the gastronome from the Crete Senesi, who is passionate about chick pea bake.
Alessia Morabito and Paola Mencarelli experiment with vegan cuisine together to create a panino with its roots in their homelands.

The campagna and riviera panino

Paola Colucci,
chef of the "Pianostrada" bistro in Rome

Bread with pumpkin seeds

salt

white pepper

black pepper

extra-virgin olive oil, for seasoning

5-6 basil leaves

½ Tropea onion

50 g Reggiano parmesan

1 burratina

Cut the aubergine into thick slices, grill and season with 2 teaspoons extra-virgin olive oil, salt and a little white pepper.
Cut the tomato into thin slices, place on a baking tray lined with greaseproof paper with a little salt and a drizzle of oil, and put in the oven at 200°C for 10 minutes.
Cut the Tropea onion into thin slices and cook gently with 2 dessertspoons of oil, a pinch of salt, pepper and a little water for 15 minutes.
Cut the basil Julienne-style.
Crumble the burrata and dry its milk.
Create the roll by alternating aubergine, parmesan, tomato, Tropea onion, basil and burrata, followed by another layer.
Finish with the basil leaves, parmesan shavings and a drizzle of extra-virgin olive oil.

bread with
pumpkin seeds

1 black
aubergine

1 hard red
tomato

Paola Colucci

Bread with pumpkin seeds

Pietro Leemann,
chef of the "Joia" restaurant in Milan

Joia

pumpernickel

kale

almond and
yuzu curd

borlotti
bean paté

bergamot and
almond curd

Pumpernickel

125 g natural starter dough

5 g koji

125 g dry buckwheat (put to soak before cooking)

60 g dry rye (put to soak before cooking)

2 prunes

50 g walnuts

80 g mixed seeds (poppy, sunflower and pumpkin)

300 g grated apple

500 g spelt flour

100 – 150 g water

12 g salt

6 g sugar

Put the rye to soak for 24 hours; drain and then boil for an hour in salted water. Boil the buckwheat for 14 minutes in salted water; drain and dry well.
Finely cut the prunes, walnuts and the seeds.
Add the koji to the starter dough and keep for 2 hours at room temperature, then place in a blender with the flour and blend for 30 seconds. In a bowl, season the apple with salt and sugar. Mix well until the water is released. Add the prunes, seeds and the walnuts, mix well. Bring the dough together with the buckwheat and rye, and work until you get a dry mixture. Finally add the water to moisten it. Put into a small cake mould, cover with cling film and leave at room temperature for 12/14 hours.
Pre-heat the oven to 210°C, remove the cling film, place in the oven and cook for 12 minutes, then lower the oven temperature to 180°C and continue cooking for 28 minutes. Finally, lower the oven temperature again to 150°C and cook for another 40 minutes. Once cooking time is complete, remove from the oven and leave to cool at room temprature.

Borlotti bean paté

Leave 40g dried borlotti beans to soak overnight. Cook them in plenty of salted water, then drain, putting aside the cooking water. Transfer them to an electric whisk bowl together with a drop of extra-virgin olive oil, a pinch of salt, a few dessertspoons of cauliflower purée and a little cooking water, and work until the desired consistency is achieved. For the cauliflower purée, boil 450 g frozen cauliflower tops in salted water. In the meantime, heat a teaspoon of finely chopped garlic, 25 ml coconut oil, 125 ml coconut milk, salt and pepper. Drain the cauliflower then blend it, adding the liquid mixture and mixing well.

Almond curd

200 g peeled dried almonds

1 l water

40 g lemon juice

1 pinch salt

Leave the almonds to soak overnight, then blend them and filter through a piece of linen. In this way you will obtain almond milk, which you will then pour into a small pan and bring to 80°C (switch off the heat as soon as bubbles appear). Add salt, mix and curdle with the lemon. Switch off the heat and cover for 30 minutes. Allow to drip through another piece of linen and transfer to a mould positioned above a draining recipient. Place in the fridge covered with a cloth for 36 hours.

Starting with the almond curd, add water, yuzu juice and salt to obtain a smooth emulsion.

Follow the same procedure to create a second emulsion substituting the yuzu juice with a little spicy bergamot paste and a touch of fermented habanero chilli pepper.

Putting the sandwich together

Fill the pumpernickel with the kale, which you have lightly fried in a drizzle of extra-virgin olive oil, cover with a second slice of bread and another layer of kale, close with the last slice of pumpernickel. Cut into small rectangles and spread them with the borlotti bean paté then the almond curd with yuzu, followed by the bergamot and habanero.

Pietro Leemann

Riccardo Monco,
chef of the "Pinchiorri" wine bar in Florence

Ciabatta with nettles, potato mortadella and pepper chutney

Ciabatta

For 5 ciabatta rolls
125 g type 00 flour
60 g water
5 g salt
7 g baking yeast
20 g parboiled nettles
1 finely chopped garlic clove
10 g cornflour

Mix a dough, with all the ingredients except the nettles and the cornflour, for 3 minutes and then leave to rest for a quarter of an hour.
Work for another 5 minutes until a smooth, shiny dough is obtained, which you then leave to rise for about an hour.
Incorporate the nettles, without over-working, on a table lightly greased with olive oil, in order to give the dough a piebald colour.
Form 5 small ciabatta rolls, leave to rise for another 40 minutes and dust with the cornflour. Bake in the oven at 235°C for 18 minutes and then put aside.

Potato mortadella

1 kg white mountain potatoes
200 g beetroot
4 l water
400 g celeriac
100 g Bronte pistachio nuts
10 g black peppercorns
50 g powdered vegetarian gelatine
14 g agar agar
salt

Peel and wash the potatoes and beetroot; cook in salted water.
Blend all the ingredients and add salt if necessary.
Clean the celeriac, cut into irregular cubes and blanche in salted water. Cool and put aside.
Add the celeriac to the potato and beetroot mixture, followed by the agar agar and the powdered gelatine: cook in a pan for about 5 minutes. Add the pistachio nuts and the pepper, leave to cool and then form a large mortadella-shaped sausage, using cling film to help you. Leave to rest overnight.

Red pepper chutney

2 peppers
100 g onion
30 g sultanas
30 g mustard seeds
30 g cane sugar
a drizzle of extra-virgin olive oil

The day before, cook the peppers on a baking tray at 220°C for about 40 minutes, then cover with cling film and put aside. When they are tepid, peel them, remove the seeds and cut into strips.
Cut the onions julienne-style and simmer in a casserole dish with the oil. Add the peppers and sugar and cook for about 20 minutes, adding the sultanas and the mustard seeds.

For the panino

a few tender Iceberg lettuce leaves
extra-virgin olive oil, for seasoning
fine dill leaves
1 handful of pistachio nuts

Cut the ciabatta roll and fill it with the mechanically sliced potato mortadella, salad leaves, chutney, a drop of oil and the dill leaves. Garnish with pistachio crumbs.

Riccardo Monco,
Italo Bassi and Annie Feolde

A panino?>>Why not!!!When Alessandro asked us, we questioned ourselves as to how we could interpret this great classic, that quick bite that nowadays we are all obliged to have, given the frenetic lifestyle that we follow. But there lies the secret: even if it is quick, it should be a healthy meal that gives us a bit of a thrill. Inspired by his shop "ino, we have tried to keep faith with his philosophy. :-)

Sesame, aubergine, lovage and chia seed panino

mixed salad of
aromatic herbs

lovage

emulsion of lovage
and chia seeds

miso
cream

chia
seeds

6 small
ciabatta rolls
with sesame
seeds

baked aubergine
with miso cream

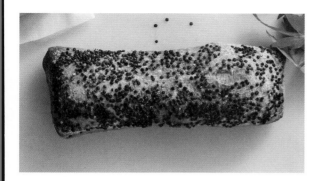

Sesame ciabatta rolls

For 6 small ciabatta rolls
120 g natural starter dough
1,2 kg type 00 flour
7 g baking yeast
850 g filtered water
28 g salt
50 g filtered water
40 g toasted sesame seeds
semolina flour

Mix all the ingredients, except the 50g filtered water, the sesame seeds and the semolina flour, in a mixer with the blade speed at 1 for about 1 minute until a rough dough is obtained. Leave to rest for 10 minutes. Blend again at the first speed setting for 5 minutes and allow to rest for another 10 minutes. Now work at the second speed setting, adding 50g water, and continue for about 8 minutes, until the mixture comes away from the sides and is very elastic.
Allow to rest for 5 minutes. Add the sesame seeds at the second speed setting for about 1 minute, transfer the mixture to a deep baking tray that has been greased with olive oil, and allow to rise at 25°C for 40/60 minutes. Then fold 3 times and leave to rise for another 40/60 minutes. Turn out onto the worktop with plenty of semolina flour underneath, spread out the dough without squashing it to form a large rectangle of even thickness and sprinkle some semola over the top. With a thin spatula make the shape of a ciabatta, turn each one over and place on greaseproof paper. Cover with cling film and allow to rise for another 20/30 minutes. Bake in the oven at 250°C with 3 minutes of steam – switch off the oven. Then steam again, and leave for 3 minutes in the oven, still off. Then switch the oven on and continue to bake for another 5 minutes until the ciabatta rolls become a dark golden colour.

For the miso cream:
80 g white miso
20 g Dijon mustard
20 g hazelnut paste
40 g hazelnut oil
40 g extra-virgin olive oil

For the lovage and chia seed emulsion:
15 g mustard seeds
50 g lovage (parboiled in water and well drained)
40 g water
60 g grape seed oil
20 g extra-virgin olive oil
salt
black pepper
20 g tofu
5 g chia seeds

Other ingredients:
2 purple aubergines
candied lemon zest for marinating with its juice
mix of aromatic herbs including coriander, dill, mint, rocket and pimpernel
1 sesame ciabatta roll

FOR THE MISO CREAM. Blend all the ingredients until a balanced cream is obtained.
FOR THE AUBERGINE. Steam the aubergine for 30 minutes. Cut into 3 cm slices and steam for another 5 minutes. Spread the miso cream on the top in a layer of about 3 mm and cook in the oven at 120°C for about 30 minutes. Remove from the oven and set aside.
FOR THE LOVAGE AND CHIA SEED EMULSION. Blend all the ingredients except the chia seeds and the oils. Bring together gradually pouring in the oils and, once the desired density has been reached, add the chia seeds, leaving the mixture to rest for at least 2 hours.
FINISHING AND PUTTING TOGETHER. Cut the small sesame ciabatta roll, spread with the lovage emulsion, place the mixed aromatic herbs on the base and add a few pieces of candied lemon zest. To conclude, add some cut slices of gently warmed aubergine on top of the mixed herbs, close the roll and serve.

Roy·Caceres.

Sesame, aubergine, lovage and chia seed panino

dried Senise peppers (so precious they are known by many as Zafrani... saffron)

Vito Mollica, *Executive Chef of the Four Seasons hotels in Florence and Milan*

The lucano panino

smoked scamorza cheese

Rotonda beans (try them and let me know what you think)

naturally leavened bread

eggs

extra-virgin olive oil

They are all products you can find in your store cupboard, which do not need to be preseved in the fridge... how lovely that world is :-)

Remove the seeds from the peppers, wash in plenty of water and dry them. Lightly fry them in plenty of olive oil until they become fleshy, add the eggs and cook until they are well combined with the peppers. Slice and toast the bread and then create a *imbiottito* (as we say in Lucano dialect) – fill with the peppers and eggs, the scamorza cheese and the bean cream. Vegetarian? Well, in this *muzzico* (bread roll in Lucano dialect) I can taste the best protein in the world... ahahahahah!

Vito Mollica

This panino is exactly what a Lucano farmer eats in order to enjoy rich and intense flavours that repay him for his hard work digging the ground by hand, inch by inch...
Oh yes, my father experienced farming just like this - only food and wine managed to bring a smile to his face once or twice a day.

1 handful Sicilian broccoli

1 pinch salt and pepper

bread

2 dessertspoons extra-virgin olive oil

220 g chick pea flour

fresh chilli pepper

100 ml water

1 clove garlic

Luisanna Messeri, *not just a chef*

My·really·really·good·panino·

To make a good chick pea bake, once you have sifted the flour you must mix it with water, a dessertspoon of oil and a pinch of salt and pepper, then leave it to rest for at least 12 hours.
When you wish to prepare your roll, take a small pan, grease it with a little oil and put on the hob. Cook the chick pea wafers as you would an omelette, one stir at a time, turning them over after a couple of minutes. They are best thin and crunchy.

If, however, you do not wish to hang around with a fish slice, you can cook it in the oven, as I have done, and even if you do not have a classic copper baking tray, cover a tray with greaseproof paper, grease it really well with good oil and pour in your mixture. Another drizzle of oil, a pinch of salt and a sprinkling of black pepper, then cook at 170°C for half an hour until it begins to colour and crack on the top. It's ready!

For the bread? In Livorno, we use salted "French" bread. You can choose whichever bread you prefer and fill it really well with your chick pea bake, without forgetting, I insist, the classic drizzle of extra-virgin olive oil and a dusting of milled black pepper. I often add a handful of Sicilian broccoli which have been boiled and then lightly fried with a little oil, a finely chopped clove of garlic and a touch of fresh chilli pepper, to my lovely rolls...

Chick pea bake, often called cake, is Livorno's great speciality, the mighty cinque e cinque (five and five) bread and cake. Livorno street food from days gone by. Prepared with chick pea flour which must be fresh, it has the same origins as the piadina and the schiacciata.
We are, to be clear, in the same world as "pane e panelle" (fritters) which you eat in Palermo, or the Genoese "farinata": even in the kitchen it's a small world! I know it seems almost impossible, but chick pea flour cooked in this way becomes a surprising, light, fragranced filling for a special panino, which makes for an exciting eating experience that you will never get bored of. Why don't you try it?
P.S.: if you don't believe me, ask Alessandro! When Irene and I took the photos at 'ino, I don't know how but he managed to wolf them down in a flash... Frassica, you're a greedyguts!

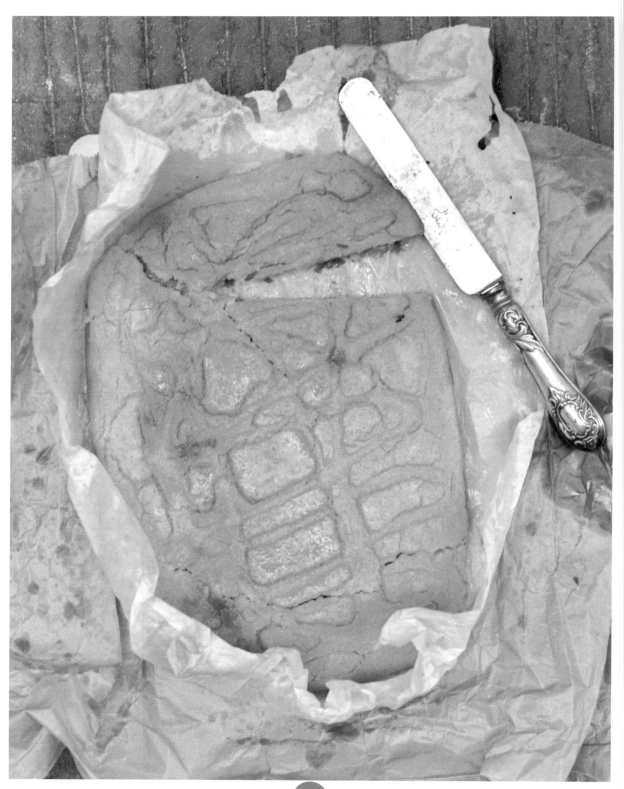

My really really good panino

Marco Stabile, *chef of the "Ora d'Aria" restaurant in Florence*

My vegetable road

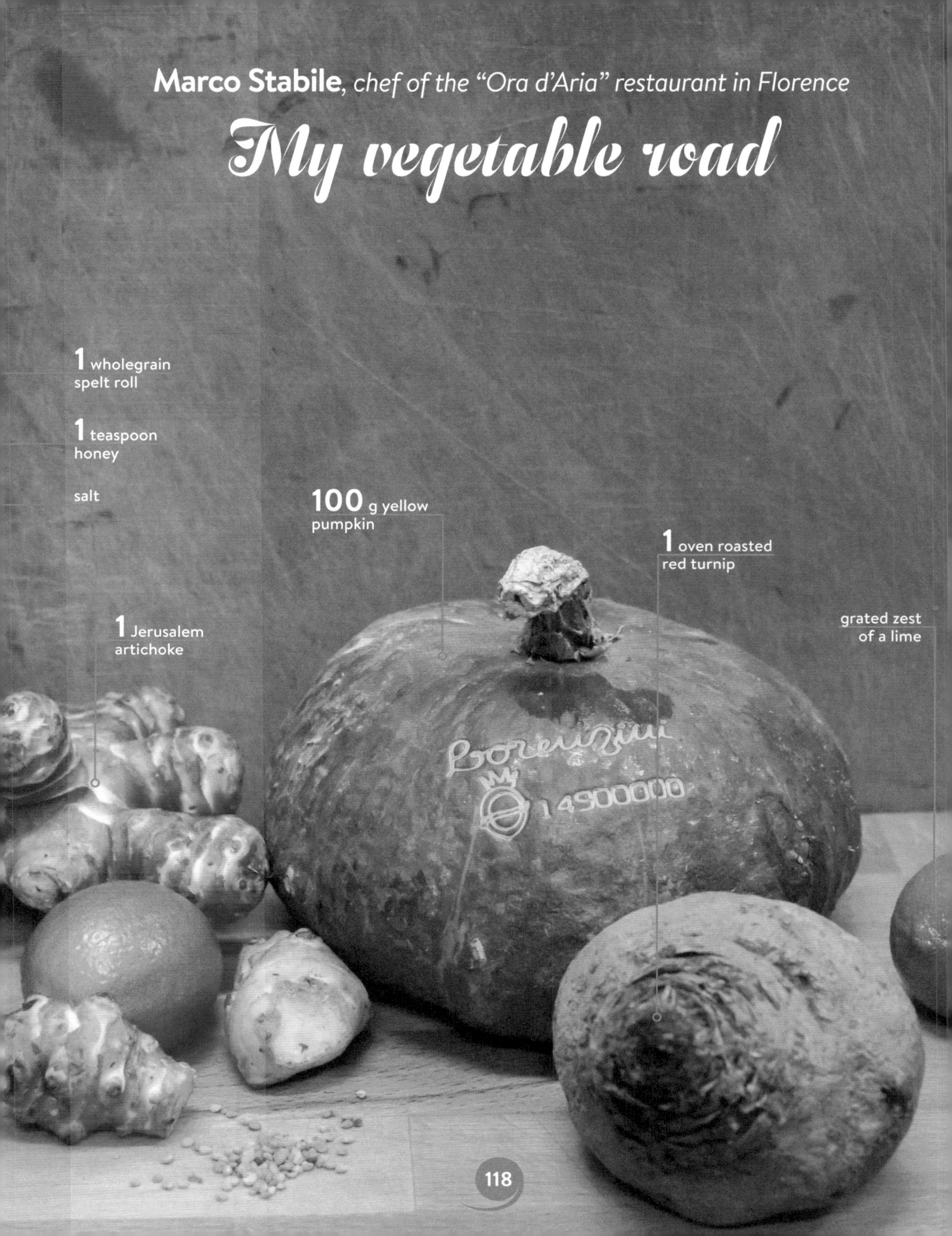

1 wholegrain spelt roll

1 teaspoon honey

salt

100 g yellow pumpkin

1 oven roasted red turnip

1 Jerusalem artichoke

grated zest of a lime

Cut the Jerusalem artichoke into thin slices with a peeler. Leave in cold water for half an hour, dry and then fry at a low temperature (120°C) until they are just golden. Place on absorbent kitchen paper and allow to dry in a warm place. Make a "mustard" by cooking the yellow pumpkin with the honey, lime zest, a little water and a pinch of salt until it becomes very soft. Reduce to make a cream. Cut the red turnip into fine slices and season. Spread the bottom half of the roll with the pumpkin mustard and cover with slices of turnip and the Jerusalem artichoke chips. Eat straight away, while the chips are very crunchy.

Marco Stabile

My vegetable road

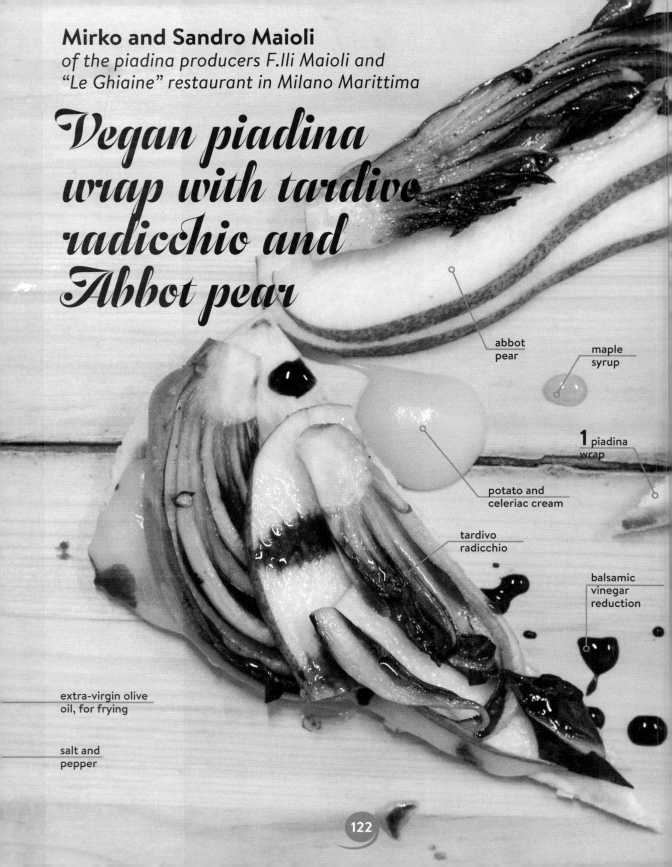

Mirko and Sandro Maioli
of the piadina producers F.lli Maioli and "Le Ghiaine" restaurant in Milano Marittima

Vegan piadina wrap with tardivo radicchio and Abbot pear

abbot
pear

maple
syrup

1 piadina
wrap

potato and
celeriac cream

tardivo
radicchio

balsamic
vinegar
reduction

extra-virgin olive
oil, for frying

salt and
pepper

Balsamic reduction

250 g balsamic vinegar
60 g sugar

Allow to boil and reduce the vinegar with the sugar. On cooling it becomes a glaze.

Potato and celeriac cream

50 g potatoes
100 g celeriac
1 small shallot
a drizzle of extra-virgin olive oil
vegetable stock
salt and pepper

Gently fry the shallot with the oil in a casserole dish, then add the cubed potatoes and celeriac. Cook in a little vegetable stock for 5 minutes. Once the vegetables are cooked, work them in an electric food mixer and check seasoning with salt and pepper.

Wash the radicchio under running water. Dry and lightly fry it in a non-stick pan with a drizzle of oil, salt and pepper.
Then lay it on the piadina wrap and add the potato and celeriac cream, the balsamic reduction, the maple syrup and the thinly sliced pear. Buon appetito.

Mirko and Sandro Maioli

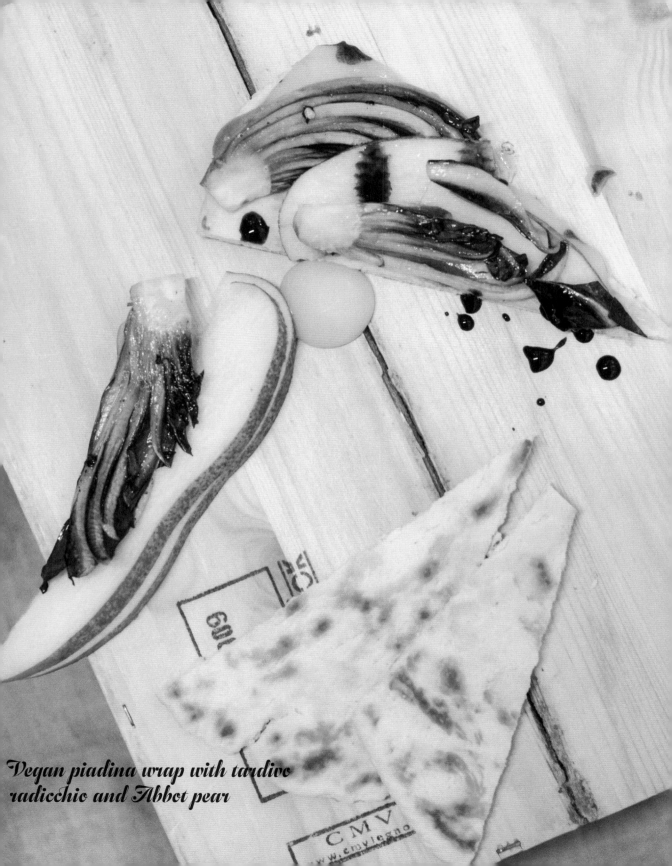

Vegan piadina wrap with tardivo radicchio and Abbot pear

Paolo Gori, *chef of the "Da Burde" trattoria in Florence*

Zolfino bean and kale pesto roll

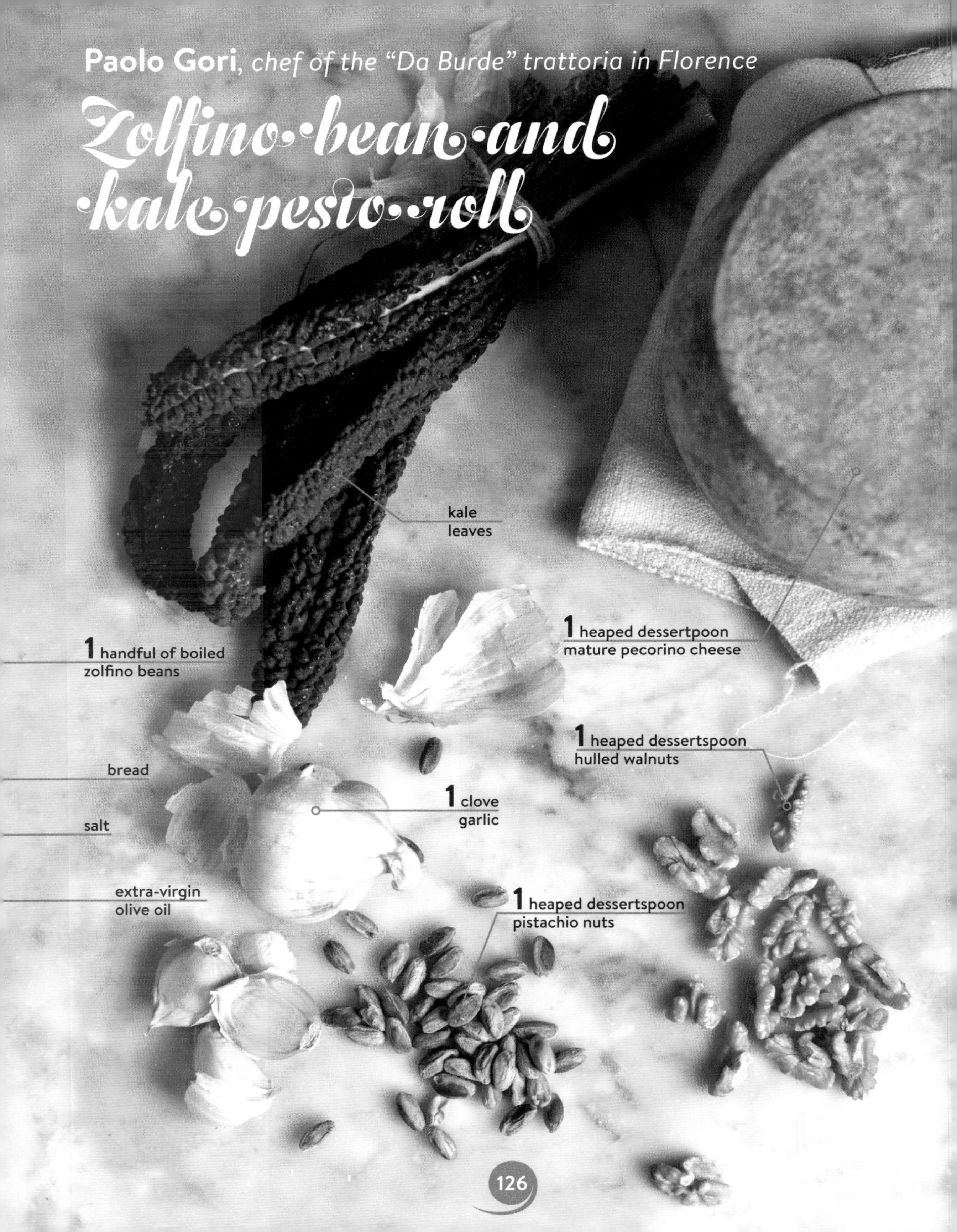

kale leaves
1 heaped dessertpoon mature pecorino cheese
1 handful of boiled zolfino beans
1 heaped dessertspoon hulled walnuts
bread
1 clove garlic
salt
extra-virgin olive oil
1 heaped dessertspoon pistachio nuts

Kale pesto

Remove the hard stem of the kale. Cut the kale into strips and parboil in slightly acidic water with the garlic for a few minutes. Drain and allow to cool. Toast the hulled walnuts in a little oil. Put everything together in a food mixer and reduce to a fine crumb. Add the mature pecorino (a mixed sheep/goat's cheese is preferable), adjust the seasoning and flavour with extra-virgin olive oil.

Lightly toast the two halves of the bread roll. Reduce the zolfino beans to a purée. Mix with a drizzle of oil and a pinch of salt. Spread 3 dessertspoons of the mixture on a slice of bread, adding a spoonful of kale pesto. Chop the pistachio nuts into medium/large pieces and spread on the top. Close with the other half of the hot bread roll.

Paolo Gori

Zolfino bean and kale pesto roll

basil

Pasquale Torrente,
chef of the "Al Convento" restaurant in Cetara

Rock in Cetara

80 g grated monk's
provolone cheese

1 nocerino
shallot

1 hamburger
roll

extra-virgin olive
oil, for seasoning

salt

Cook the potatoes in their skins for 40 minutes, then cut them into cubes. Put the shallot, the potatoes and the courgettes cut into small cubes into a pan and lightly cook, adding a little salt. Add the provolone cheese and the basil; cream well. Use a pasta cutter to make hamburger shapes which you then place on kitchen paper and leave in the fridge for 2 hours.
Fill the rolls with the hamburgers adding the milk cream, a little more basil and a drizzle of oil.
Buon appetito amici miei!

600 g
courgettes

300 g
potatoes

100 g Monti
Lattari milk cream

Pasquale Torrente

Rock in Cetara

Cristina Bowerman,
chef of the "Glass" and the "Romeo" restaurants in Rome

Pitta bread filled with vegetarian mushroom ragù

4 pitta breads
1 finely sliced white onion
400 g roughly chopped champignon mushrooms
200 g shiitake mushrooms
30 g white wine
30 g white vinegar
100 g roughly chopped taggiasca (or Gaeta) olives
1 handful pine nuts
40 g plump sultanas soaked in hot water
1 bunch thyme
1 handful finely chopped parsley
garlic oil

salt

Sweat the onion in a casserole dish, turning constantly.
In a pan, lightly fry the mushrooms in a little garlic oil and
add them to the onion.
Blend with the white wine and the vinegar and cook the
mushrooms as for a ragù, then add the olives. When
the cooking time is almost complete, add the pine nuts,
sultanas, thyme and parsley, season and leave to cool.
Warm the pitta breads and remove the crumb. Fill with hot
ragù and serve.

Cristina Bowerman

Pitta bread filled with vegetarian mushroom ragù

Index

Analytical index

Alphabetical index

Acknowledgements

A book of healthy panini, made by "healthy" people, to whom I am truly grateful.
Thank you to the staff of 'ino: Serena, Hiroko, Lucrezia and Paola.
Thanks to Fulvio Marino, for his precious contributions on the theme of flour, and to the Marino family.
Thanks to Francesco Barthel and the staff of Desinare.
Thanks to Irene Berni for the warm welcome at her B&B Valdirose and, naturally, to all chefs and friends who participated and lent us their locations with great collaboration and enthusiasm.

Alessandro Frassica, owner of the 'ino restaurant in Florence, is back, following the great success of his first book "the PAN'INO", from Guido Tommasi Editore.
With 'ino, the sandwich becomes a storytelling tool. Everything begins with research and the choice of top quality ingredients, the fruits of numerous journeys and tastings. Behind every ingredient there is a land, a tradition and people whose talents have been recognised by Alessandro, with simplicity and passion, transforming himself into a "panino chef" and taking his creations around the world.

© Guido Tommasi Editore – Datanova S.r.l., 2016

Text: Alessandro Frassica
Photographs: Irene Berni
Graphics: Tommaso Bacciocchi
Translation: Lucy Howell
Editorial: Anita Ravasio

ISBN: 978 88 6753 167 7

Printed in Italy